Keep It SIMPLE, Rapunzel!

The Fairy-Tale Physics of Simple Machines

by Thomas Kingsley Troupe

illustrated by Jomike Tejido

PICTURE WINDOW BOOKS
a capstone imprint

A little while back, in a place you've never visited, lived a witch. Her name was Dame Gothel. She grew the most amazing vegetables in her garden. One day she caught her neighbor stealing a handful of turnips. The man said his wife loved turnips. If he didn't bring her some to eat, she would die.

Dame Gothel told the man he could have as many turnips as he wanted—on one condition. The couple had to give her their first baby. The man agreed. And a few months after his daughter was born, the witch snatched her away.

"I should call you Turnip," Dame Gothel told the baby. "But I'm going to call you Rapunzel, instead. Just because."

Like other kids, Rapunzel enjoyed singing, reading books, and kickboxing. Unlike other kids, she spent every day locked in a tall tower. Rapunzel was never allowed to come down. And she never saw more than her own backyard.

Years went by. Rapunzel's hair grew long and strong.
It was long enough for Dame Gothel to climb up.

"Rapunzel, Rapunzel, let down your hair!" the witch called.

"OK!" Rapunzel said. She hung her hair on a hook outside
her window. Dame Gothel grabbed it and started climbing.

Little did they know, a prince named Dave was watching. He'd driven past the tower many times before. He wondered about the girl living in it.

"So that's how the witch gets up there," Prince Dave said. "Huh. She should build a ramp or some steps."

Prince Dave sometimes watched farmers push their carts up the ramps at his castle. The royal carpenters called the ramps a type of simple machine. Simple machines, they said, made work easier.

PRINCE MOBILE

Prince Dave really wanted to meet Rapunzel. He waited until Dame Gothel left. Then, when the coast was clear, he snuck over to the tower. In his witchiest voice, he called, "Rapunzel, Rapunzel, let down your hair!"

"Why?" Rapunzel called without looking out the window. "You were just up here."

Again in his witchy voice, Prince Dave said, "Yes, I know, dear. I think I lost a contact lens in your room."

He wasn't sure his plan would work.

"Fine," Rapunzel said with a sigh. She dropped down her hair. "Come on up."

In a few minutes, Prince Dave appeared at the window. Rapunzel gasped.

"Hey!" she shouted. "Who are you?"

"I'm Prince Dave. But please, call me Dave," he replied.

No one besides Dame Gothel had ever entered the tower before. Rapunzel put up her fists.

"Whoa!" Prince Dave said. "I'm not going to hurt you. I just wanted to meet you."

"Oh," Rapunzel said. "Well, my name's Rapunzel. I don't get many visitors—none, actually, except Dame Gothel."

"So the witch keeps you locked up in here?" Prince Dave asked.

Rapunzel nodded. "My whole life so far," she said. "I mean, the tower's nice and all. I read *a lot*. But I want to *see* the world, not just read about it."

Prince Dave smiled. "Then let's get you out of here," he said.

Rapunzel gave the prince a quick tour of her room. She showed him her books, guitars, and kickboxing bag.

"How did you hang that heavy bag?" Prince Dave asked.

"Easy," Rapunzel said. "I used a screw."

Prince Dave scratched his head. He was confused.

Rapunzel grabbed a spare screw from her desk drawer and held it up. "You see, a screw is a simple machine," she explained. "It's an inclined plane—like a ramp—wrapped around a cylinder. The ridges are called threads. When you twist a screw into a piece of wood, the ridges hold it in place."

Prince Dave nodded. "OK, sure," he said. "And the pointy tip makes the screw go into the wood easier."

"Nailed it," Rapunzel said. "Ha! I guess that sounded kind of screwy, huh?" She smiled, then giggled.

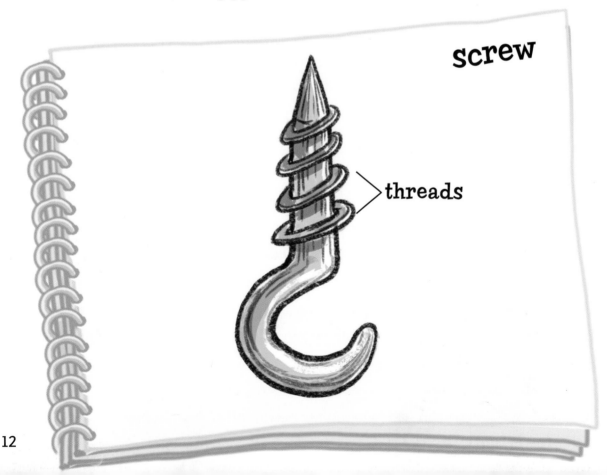

screw

threads

Prince Dave wanted to show Rapunzel the world. And Rapunzel wanted to see it.

"I'll get some tools," the prince said. He started to climb down her hair. "I'll build something to get you out of here."

When he reached the ground, a turnip hit him in the head. Dame Gothel ran toward him, pushing a cart of turnips.

"You!" she shouted. "Get out of here!"

Prince Dave ducked as another turnip flew at him. He watched the witch push the cart. The wheel and axle made it easier for her to move the heavy load.

"Hey, Rapunzel!" Prince Dave called. "The wheel and axle on that cart . . . are they another type of simple machine?"

"Yes!" Rapunzel shouted. "Now run!"

The young prince ran off, and Dame Gothel climbed up Rapunzel's hair.

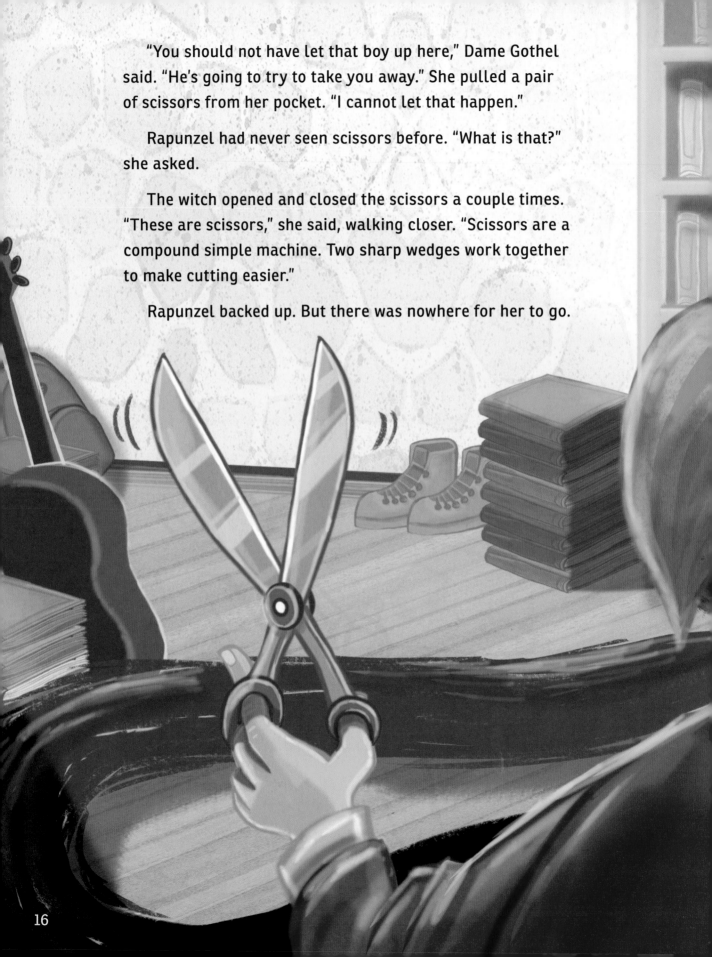

"You should not have let that boy up here," Dame Gothel said. "He's going to try to take you away." She pulled a pair of scissors from her pocket. "I cannot let that happen."

Rapunzel had never seen scissors before. "What is that?" she asked.

The witch opened and closed the scissors a couple times. "These are scissors," she said, walking closer. "Scissors are a compound simple machine. Two sharp wedges work together to make cutting easier."

Rapunzel backed up. But there was nowhere for her to go.

Early the next morning, Prince Dave returned with his toolbox. "Rapunzel," he called quietly, "I brought some tools. Let down your hair so we can get you out of here!"

A few long strands of hair fell at the prince's feet. The problem? Rapunzel wasn't attached to them anymore.

Rapunzel peeked shyly out the window. "Dame Gothel cut my hair!" she cried.

Prince Dave thought the new haircut looked pretty good. "Don't worry," he said. "I've got all kinds of ideas."

Prince Dave set down his toolbox . . . and it quickly sunk in the mud. He tried to pull it out, but it wouldn't budge.

Rapunzel leaned forward. "What's going on down there?" she asked.

"My tools are stuck in the mud," the prince answered.

Rapunzel pointed at the fence around the witch's garden. "Grab one of those boards and set it on that rock," she said. "Then wiggle one end under your toolbox."

Prince Dave did as he was told.

lever

beam

fulcrum

"Now push down on the other end of the board," Rapunzel continued. "Your toolbox should lift out easily from the mud."

Again, Prince Dave did as he was told. With a push, he freed his toolbox. "Well," he said, "now how did that—"

"It's another simple machine, Dave," Rapunzel explained. "I read about it. It's called a lever. The board is the beam, and the rock is the fulcrum. Easy peasy."

Rapunzel checked the clock. The prince was taking too long. Dame Gothel would be coming soon with breakfast.

"What's the plan, Dave?" she called.

Prince Dave scratched his head. "I want to build something," he said. "But I didn't bring any wood. And the fence boards aren't thick enough."

"Did you bring an ax?" Rapunzel asked.

Prince Dave opened his toolbox. He showed her the small ax he had.

"Perfect," Rapunzel said. "An ax is a type of wedge. Wedges are simple machines, and they—"

"Let me guess," the prince said, walking over to a nearby tree. "They make work easier?"

"That's right," Rapunzel said. "Get chopping!"

Prince Dave chopped down the tree. Then he chopped down another tree.

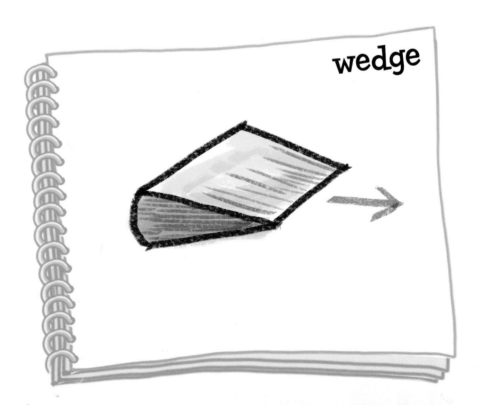

wedge

A short time later, the prince had shaped the trees into planks.

"Pack your bags, m'lady!" he called to Rapunzel. "I'm building you a ramp!"

"Yet another simple machine," Rapunzel said. "A ramp is an inclined plane. It makes it easier to move objects to different levels."

Prince Dave built the ramp while Rapunzel gathered her things. But he hadn't cut nearly enough wood. The ramp reached only partway up the tower.

"Sorry about that," he said.

"No problem," Rapunzel said. She tossed three suitcases out the window. They landed on the ramp and slid down.

"Well, the ramp worked for your luggage," Prince Dave said. "But what about you? You can't just throw yourself onto the ramp like a suitcase."

Rapunzel's face brightened. She had an idea. "We should build an elevator," she said. "I've got a pulley up here. Pulleys are a type of—"

"Simple machine!" the prince said.

"Yes!" Rapunzel cried. "Pulleys make it easier to raise and lower loads."

Prince Dave shook his head. "Seriously, how do you know so much about physics?" he asked.

Rapunzel smiled, then dropped a box full of books onto the ramp.

"I've been locked in a tower my whole life, Dave," she said. "Like I said, I read a lot!"

Prince Dave built a small seat. While he did that, Rapunzel attached the pulley to the beam above her window.

"Wait!" the prince said. "One problem. I don't have any rope!"

Rapunzel held out the rest of the long hair that had been cut from her head. "I'm way ahead of you," she said.

Rapunzel threw her long hair over the pulley. The prince attached one end of the braid to the seat. When he pulled the other end, the seat rose into the air! Rapunzel hopped on, and Prince Dave quickly lowered her to freedom.

But there was trouble!

"Uh-oh," Prince Dave said. "Here comes the witch!"

Dame Gothel was running across the yard. She shouted and threw turnips.

Rapunzel and the prince picked everything up and raced to the waiting car. They couldn't wait to live happily ever after.

"Rapunzel! Come back here!" Dame Gothel yelled. "You won't escape that easily!"

"I just did," Rapunzel said. "And with the help of simple machines? It *was* easy!"

Glossary

axle—a rod in the center of a wheel around which the wheel turns

compound—having two or more parts

cylinder—a shape with flat, circular ends and sides shaped like a tube

inclined plane—a slanting surface, like a ramp, that is used to move objects to different levels; two inclined planes form a wedge

lever—a beam resting on a pivot point (fulcrum) that is used to lift objects when pressure is applied to the other end

physics—the science that deals with matter and energy; physics includes the study of light, heat, sound, electricity, motion, and force

pulley—a grooved wheel turned by a rope, belt, or chain that is used to move heavy objects

screw—a cylinder with an inclined plane running around the outside that can be twisted into something to hold it in place

simple machine—a tool with one or no moving parts that moves an object when you push or pull; inclined planes, wheels and axles, levers, pulleys, screws, and wedges are examples of simple machines

wedge—two inclined planes that are used to split things apart or push them together

Critical Thinking Questions

1. Look at the illustration on pages 2 and 3. Find at least three simple machines and explain how they make work easier.

2. Name two simple machines in your classroom. How would you get your work done if these simple machines didn't exist?

Read More

Oxlade, Chris. *Making Machines with Levers.* Simple Machines Projects. Chicago: Capstone Raintree, 2015.

Schuh, Mari. *Making a Salad: Wedge vs. Inclined Plane.* Simple Machines to the Rescue. Minneapolis: Lerner Publications, 2016.

Weakland, Mark. *Smash!: Wile E. Coyote Experiments with Simple Machines.* Wile E. Coyote, Physical Science Genius. North Mankato, Minn.: Capstone Press, an imprint of Capstone Press, 2014.

Internet Sites

Use FactHound to find Internet sites related to this book.

Visit *www.facthound.com*

Just type in 9781515828952 and go.

Look for all the books in the series!

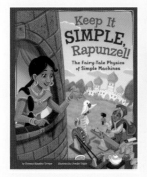

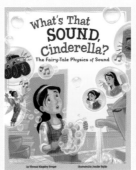

Index

Special thanks to our adviser, Darsa Donelan, Professor of Physics, Gustavus Adolphus College, Saint Peter, Minnesota, for her expertise.

Editor: Jill Kalz
Designer: Lori Bye
Premedia Specialist: Tori Abraham
The illustrations in this book were created digitally.

Picture Window Books
1710 Roe Crest Drive
North Mankato, MN 56003
www.mycapstone.com

Library of Congress Cataloging-in-Publication data is available on the Library of Congress website.
ISBN: 978-1-5158-2895-2 (library binding)
ISBN: 978-1-5158-2899-0 (paperback)
ISBN: 978-1-5158-2903-4 (eBook PDF)
Summary: Escaping from a tall tower using one's hair is SO fairy-tale old school. THIS STEM-smart Rapunzel uses the brain beneath her hair to educate her prince (and readers) on the ways the science of simple machines can save the day.

Printed and bound in the United States of America.
PA021